ALL ABOUT MY

MW01298150

BY: ______________________

SCHOOL NAME: ______________________

MY PRINCIPAL'S NAME IS

____

THE BEST THING ABOUT MY PRINCIPAL IS:

____

____

____

____

____

____

____

THANK YOU FOR BEING A GREAT PRINCIPAL